**work
pers**

AND
BLITZ

*by Alice Proctor
Consultant: Alison Howard*

How to use this book

Each topic in this book is clearly labelled and contains all these components:

Topic heading

Introduction to the topic

Sub-topic 1 offers complete information about one aspect of the topic

Words in capitals are explained in the Glossary

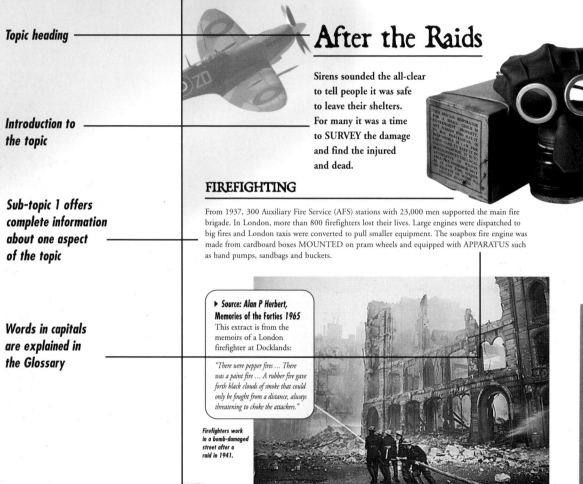

After the Raids

Sirens sounded the all-clear to tell people it was safe to leave their shelters. For many it was a time to SURVEY the damage and find the injured and dead.

FIREFIGHTING

From 1937, 300 Auxiliary Fire Service (AFS) stations with 23,000 men supported the main fire brigade. In London, more than 800 firefighters lost their lives. Large engines were dispatched to big fires and London taxis were converted to pull smaller equipment. The soapbox fire engine was made from cardboard boxes MOUNTED on pram wheels and equipped with APPARATUS such as hand pumps, sandbags and buckets.

▶ **Source: Alan P Herbert, Memories of the Forties 1965**
This extract is from the memoirs of a London firefighter at Docklands:

"There were pepper fires ... There was a paint fire ... A rubber fire gave forth black clouds of smoke that could only be fought from a distance, always threatening to choke the attackers."

Firefighters work in a bomb-damaged street after a raid in 1941.

14

EMERGENCY SERV

A team of civil defence worker
AMBULANCE crew and str
went to the aid of those tr
wounded. Complete si
to hear any cries for h
rubble. Buildings coul
time, and burst water, ga
unexploded bombs posed f

**Respirators were handed out during r
by civil defence workers.**

▶ **Source: T P Peters, Remin**
T P Peters, an air raid wa
Grinstead, wrote about h

*"Unexploded German bombs we
The Chief Warden and I would
holes armed with rods, to enable
necessary forms, etc, for the Bom*

CASE STUDY

Air-raid wardens

Each London borough had teams of A
women. Wardens worked over 72 hou
and checking that people had gas ma
sirens, fighting fires, giving first aid

▶ **Source: T P Peters, Reminiscen**
Air-raid warden T P Peters wr

*"When the Prime Minister announced
country was well prepared with its ARI
a good training from Colonel Eaton, th*

ISBN 978 1 84898 076 1

This edition published in 2009 by *ticktock* Media Ltd

Printed in China

9 8 7 6 5 4 3 2 1

A CIP catalogue record for this book is available from the British Library.

Copyright © *ticktock* Entertainment Ltd 2005. First published in Great Britain in 2005 by *ticktock* Media Ltd, The Old Sawmill, 103 Goods Station Road, Tunbridge Wells, Kent, TN1 2DP.

Sub-topic 2 offers complete information about one aspect of the topic

Some suggested words to use in your project

The Glossary explains the meaning of any unusual or difficult words appearing on these two pages

Words to use in your project

anecdote – a short amusing story of history or biography
collected – gathered together
gash – a long, deep cut
inspection – an official examination or review
shambles – a place of carnage; a mess or muddle

Glossary

borough – a term for a town, and also a district of London
ambulance – a vehicle used for transporting sick and injured people
apparatus – equipment needed for a particular activity or purpose
mounted – placed on top of
survey – to examine carefully and thoroughly

See also: The Raids 6–7; The Shelters 12–13; The Destruction 16–17; Work and Play 20–21

Other pages in the book that relate to what you have read here are listed in this bar

The Case Study is a closer look at a famous person, artefact or building that relates to the topic

who were
the blackout
ed sounding
oded bombs.

the
ceived

A young air-raid warden in uniform.

15

Captions clearly explain what is in the picture

Each photo or illustration is described and discussed in its accompanying text

CONTENTS

The Blitz

The Blitz (a shortened version of the German word blitzkrieg, or 'lightning war') was the bombing campaign carried out on British cities and towns by the Germans during World War II.

THE BOMBINGS

The Germans started the Blitz on 7 September 1940, by bombing London. The bombing of British cities and towns would continue every day and night for 57 days. The Blitz ended on 10 May 1941, so the Germans could prepare to INVADE Russia.

> ▶ *Source: 'A Dreadful Masterpiece', Ernie's War: The Best of Ernie Pyle's World War II Dispatches, 1986.*
> CORRESPONDENT Ernie Pyle describes a night raid on London:
>
> *"They came just after dark, and somehow you could sense from the quick, bitter firing of the guns that there was to be no monkey business this night. Shortly after the sirens wailed you could hear the Germans grinding overhead."*

Luftwaffe Commander Hermann Goring (left) with Ernst Udet, who chose the force's planes.

The first mass air raid on London, 7 September 1940.

THE LUFTWAFFE

The Luftwaffe (pronounced 'looft-vaaf-feh') was the German air force, the most powerful in the world. Hermann Göring, head of the Luftwaffe, thought it would take only a month to destroy Britain's Royal Air Force (RAF). But the Luftwaffe met fierce resistance, so it changed TACTIC and its planes were sent to destroy British cities and towns instead.

> ▶ **Sources: Operation Seelöwe (Sea Lion), DIRECTIVE No. 16, 16 July 1940**
> Adolf Hitler's Directive No. 16 states:
>
> *"Since Britain still shows no sign of willingness to come to an agreement in spite of her hopeless military situation, I have decided to prepare and if necessary carry out an AMPHIBIOUS operation against England… to eliminate the English mother country as a base for continuation of the war against Germany and, if it should become necessary, to occupy the entire island."*

Words to use in your project

Axis – *the alliance between Germany, Italy and Japan during World War II*

casualty – *a dead or injured person*

command – *to order, demand or exercise control over*

infrastructure – *a basic framework; a system of communications*

rationing – *the act of limiting the food supply*

Glossary

amphibious – *involving water*

correspondent – *reporter*

directive – *an official or authorative instruction*

invade – *to enter and take over a country with an armed force*

tactic – *a system or element of skilled or calculated operations*

See also: The Raids 6–7; Evacuation 8–9; Shelters 12–13; Significant People 24–25

CASE STUDY

The Battle of Britain

In July 1940, Germany's air force, the Luftwaffe, began its attack. It tried to destroy the RAF by targeting radar bases, airfields and plane factories in preparation for a planned invasion. The Luftwaffe had more aircraft and pilots, but the RAF had better planes as well as radar and observation posts. The RAF lost 792 planes in the following three months. The Luftwaffe lost nearly twice as many.

> ▶ **Source: Speech by Winston Churchill, 20 August 1940**
> Winston Churchill praised the 3,080 pilots who had defended Britain:
>
> *"Never, in the field of human conflict, has so much been owed by so many, to so few!"*

RAF Spitfires (above) and Hurricanes proved superior aircraft to the German fighters in the Battle of Britain.

The Raids

Luftwaffe attacks during the Battle of Britain left the RAF on the point of collapse. Then Hermann Göring ordered the Luftwaffe to TARGET other towns and cities, which gave the RAF time to repair its planes. The Blitz had started. The Luftwaffe made 127 night raids on Britain. The attacks were designed to destroy important buildings, and damage MORALE.

LONDON

London was the most heavily bombed British city during the Blitz. The Luftwaffe targeted industrial areas, major ports, factories and transport links. More than 16,000 tonnes of bombs were dropped on London – more than were dropped on the whole of the rest of Britain. More than 20,000 Londoners died and 1.4 million were made homeless.

> ▶ **Source: Kingsley Martin, Father Figures, 1966**
> In his AUTOBIOGRAPHY, Kingsley Martin wrote:
>
> *"In the West End, we could 'take' the raids we got; whether we could have survived many more like the last two raids in the spring of 1941 … I don't know … but … bombs do not induce surrender."*

A typical scene of East End life in London, 1940. Life continued despite the raids.

OTHER TARGETS

The main targets outside London were Belfast, Birmingham, Bristol, Cardiff, Coventry, Glasgow, Hull, Liverpool, Manchester, Newcastle, Nottingham, Portsmouth, Plymouth, Sheffield and Southampton. All had some industrial or wartime purpose that the Germans wanted to DISABLE. But sometimes a bomber that had missed its target drop zone would simply drop bombs at random, killing innocent civilians.

> ▶ **Source: Leonard Woolf, The Journey Not the Arrival Matters, 1969**
>
> Publisher Leonard Woolf, the husband of the famous novelist Virginia, lived in Rodmell, Sussex at the start of the war, and wrote:
>
> *"The strange first air raid of the war … It came, I think, just after or before breakfast and I walked out onto the lawn which looks over the water-meadows to Lewes and the Downs."*

Words to use in your project

Barbarossa – *the code name for the German invasion of the Soviet Union in June 1941*

fighter-bomber – *an attacking/ bombing aircraft, used in tactical and defensive operations*

reconnaissance – *to survey to seek out information about enemy positions or installations*

Glossary

autobiography – *an account of a person's life written by that person*

disable – *to make inactive*

explosive – *likely to shatter violently or burst apart*

incendiaries – *devices designed to cause fires*

morale – *confidence or optimism in a person or a group*

target – *to select as an object of attack*

See also: The Blitz 4–5; Defence 10–11; Shelters 12–13; After the Raids 14–15; Women and Children 22–23

The Blitz Memorial in Liverpool. It reads: "In loving memory of the Citizens of Liverpool and Bootle who lost their lives in the Blitz of 1940–42."

CASE STUDY

Blitz on Coventry

The worst devastation outside London was in Coventry, home of some large manufacturing companies that made planes and other war items. At 7.20pm on 14 November, the first of 500 German bombers dropped INCENDIARIES to mark the way. Within 10 minutes, the second wave of bombers arrived and dropped high EXPLOSIVE bombs.

> ▶ **Source: The Guardian, 16 November 1940**
>
> A newspaper reported:
>
> *"The spire of Coventry Cathedral today stood as a sentinel over the grim scene of destruction following a dusk-to-dawn raid on the town which the Nazis claimed was the biggest attack in the history of air war."*

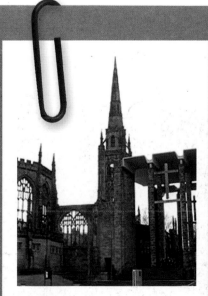

Coventry Cathedral – only the tower and outer walls remain intact today.

Evacuation

Mass EVACUATION began on the first day of the war: 3 September 1939. The evacuation involved the relocation of children, teachers, PREGNANT women, mothers with pre-school children and disabled people to the safety of the countryside.

CHILDREN

In August 1940, there was a second evacuation and a third in August 1944. Most children were evacuated in school groups with their teachers. Many had to travel for hours to get to their new homes. Some children were very unhappy.

When children arrived in the host town or village, they might be lined up in a hall so that host families could choose one of them. Sometimes a host family would already have been arranged.

▶ **Source: Extract from an interview conducted by the www.battleofbritain1940.net website**
George Clarke, an ARP (Air Raid Precautions) official at the Bethnal Green, London reception point, wrote:

"The feelings amongst the mothers was generally quite orderly, … But the children's behaviour was quite different. Some remained very quiet tightly holding onto mum's hand …"

This child waits for her new family during evacuation.

THE EVACUATION

For the purposes of evacuation, Britain was divided into three areas. Evacuation areas were urban districts that expected heavy bombing. Neutral areas neither sent nor took evacuees, while reception areas were rural areas where evacuees were sent. In total, one and a half million people took advantage of the government's evacuation SCHEME, and two million made their own arrangements.

A scene from a party for London children evacuated to Worthing.

> ▶ **Source: Extracted from an interview conducted by the www.battleofbritain1940.net website**
> This account by Ron Collins tells of his experiences as a boy during the war:
>
> *"I remember it was so different from our house in Stepney … a bathroom and an indoor LAVATORY upstairs. It was wonderful having my own towel hanging on the door, and all the toiletries were on the side next to the wash basin that even had hot water."*

Words to use in your project

asylum – *shelter or protection from danger*
charge – *to demand as a price or fee*
exodus – *the depature of a large group of people*
luggage – *suitcases, trunks*
refugee – *a person who seeks shelter elsewhere, particularly in a time of war*

Glossary

billeting – *allocating sleeping quarters for soldiers and evacuees*
evacuation – *the removal of people from a place*
lavatory – *a toilet*
pregnant – *carrying a child in the womb*
scheme – *a systematic plan of action for attaining a particular goal*

See also: The Blitz 4–5; The Raids 6–7; Destruction 16–17; Weapons 28–29; Crime 30–31

CASE STUDY

Billets

BILLETING officers found families who were willing to take in evacuees. They received 10s 6d (10 shillings and sixpence, or about 52p) from the government for one child. Many children from poor city areas had not been properly fed. As a result, the government issued free school milk, and cod liver oil for children under five.

> ▶ **Source: Voices from the Past: The Blitz, 1987**
> Evelyn Rose was evacuated from her London home when war broke out:
>
> *"I was fourteen when war was declared. We were billeted with a family in a large house where there were servants. It was not something that we were used to."*

Children having their feet inspected before evacuation.

Defence

Britain's defence was the responsibility of the armed services working with the emergency services and volunteer organizations. Early warning radar systems, anti-aircraft guns, SEARCHLIGHTS, air-raid SIRENS and BARRAGE balloons were used to combat bombing raids. The Royal Observer Corps notified ground and air defences about IMPENDING attacks.

MILITARY DEFENCE

Manned anti-aircraft guns were set up to shoot down enemy planes. Searchlights scanned the night sky for planes. Huge silver barrage balloons were flown over the countryside to prevent planes from flying low. A plane that hit a balloon or its cable would crash.

A cluster of Royal Air Force barrage balloons at Cardington, Bedfordshire.

CIVIL DEFENCE

Arrangements to protect civilians in war are known as civil defence. The war on the home front involved the Air Raid Precautions (ARP), the Royal Observer Corps and the Civil Defence Cadet Corps. First National aid teams, fire-watchers, firefighters and RESCUE parties were trained with the emergency services (fire, police and ambulance). Air-raid wardens dealt with the consequences of bombs dropped in a particular area.

A WWII air-raid siren.

▶ Source: Extract from a British government circular 'Air Raid Warnings', 1939

This excerpt is from 'Air Raid Warnings', a government circular:

"When air raids are threatened, warning will be given in towns by sirens and hooters … When you hear the warning, take cover at once … Stay under cover until you hear the sirens sounding continuously for two minutes on the same note …"

Words to use in your project

artillery – *offensive weapons of war; the branch of the military using these weapons*

camouflage – *a disguise or method of concealment*

devastate – *to ravage or destroy*

pillage – *to deprive of money or property by violence*

Glossary

barrage – *a military bombardment, a barrier*

impending – *about to happen*

rescue – *to save from a dangerous or distressing situation*

sirens – *devices that produce a loud sound, used as a warning*

searchlights – *huge spotlights, often used to find things in the air or water*

See also: The Raids 6–7; ; Work and Play 20–21; Weapons 28–29

CASE STUDY

The Blackout

A blackout was ordered so that the Luftwaffe could not use lights as targets. The blackout came into force 30 minutes after sunset until 30 minutes before sunrise. All lights, including street lamps, had to be switched off, and all windows and doors had to be covered.

▶ Source: Extract from a government circular, 1939

A government circular described the blackout law:

"All windows, skylights, glazed doors, or other openings which would show a light, will have to be screened … with dark blinds … or brown paper pasted on the glass, so that no light is visible from outside."

Government adverts told people what to do during the blackout.

Shelters

Two kinds of SHELTERS were used at home: the Anderson shelter and the Morrison shelter. In public areas, shelters were often below the ground, and in London the UNDERGROUND railway was used. Underground stations were kitted out with beds, toilets and first-aid facilities.

HOME SHELTERS

The government knew a bomb hitting a large public shelter could result in more deaths, so it encouraged families to build home shelters, which it gave out free. Anderson shelters were CONSTRUCTED from CORRUGATED metal and had to be dug 1.2 metres into the ground. An alternative was the Morrison indoor shelter. This was a large metal frame about 2 metres long and 1.2 metres wide, with wire walls.

▶ **Source: Extract from the memoirs of Muriel Sybil Ward, born in 1916**
Muriel Sybil Ward lived in East London for more than 30 years until 1948:

"My mother and I slept in an Anderson air raid shelter in the garden most nights ... My father only joined us if things 'got bad'!"

An Anderson Shelter erected in January 1940.

GOING UNDERGROUND

At the peak of the Blitz, 79 Underground stations became shelters, and up to 177,000 Londoners slept in them each night. Though they were considered safe, there were many deaths when

A reconstruction of a wartime London Underground shelter.

stations including Bank and Balham took direct hits. The London Underground was also used by the government. Special offices were built in disused passages and used by the War Cabinet and Anti-Aircraft Control.

> ▶ **Source: Extract from an interview conducted by the www.battleofbritain1940.net website**
>
> Evelyn Rose describes the Underground shelters:
>
> *"I did not like using them myself. The stench was unbearable. The smell was so bad I don't know how people did not die from SUFFOCATION. So many bodies and no fresh air coming in."*

Words to use in your project

alarm – *a signal, sound, cry, etc., that is a warning of danger*
council – *a group of people called together for consultation*
disorder – *an upset of normal function*
household – *the home and its affairs*
sanctuary – *a place of refuge*

Glossary

constructed – *built*
corrugated – *ridged and grooved*
shelters – *places that provides protection*
sing-songs – *gatherings for singing*
suffocation – *death through lack of air*
underground – *beneath the surface*

See also: The Raids 6–7; Evacuation 8–9; Defence 10–11; Women and Children 22–23

CASE STUDY

Shelter marshals

Shelter marshals kept order in public air-raid shelters. Londoners using Tube stations for overnight shelter often turned up well before the sirens went off to secure a good spot, and this could cause disagreements.

> ▶ **Source: Extract from an interview conducted by the www.battleofbritain1940.net website**
>
> Dolly Rolph, a deputy warden in shelters in Bethnal Green, saw some people bringing in a piano and having noisy SING-SONGS that kept other people awake. She had to ask the local council to restrict the noise. She said:
>
> *"They were lively times."*

Two men play harmonica in a shelter.

After the Raids

Sirens sounded the all-clear to tell people it was safe to leave their shelters. For many it was a time to SURVEY the damage and find the injured and dead.

FIREFIGHTING

From 1937, 300 Auxiliary Fire Service (AFS) stations with 23,000 men supported the main fire brigade. In London, more than 800 firefighters lost their lives. Large engines were dispatched to big fires and London taxis were converted to pull smaller equipment. The soapbox fire engine was made from cardboard boxes MOUNTED on pram wheels and equipped with APPARATUS such as hand pumps, sandbags and buckets.

▶ **Source: Alan P Herbert, Memories of the Forties, 1965**

This extract is from the memoirs of a London firefighter at Docklands:

"There were pepper fires … There was a paint fire … A rubber fire gave forth black clouds of smoke that could only be fought from a distance, always threatening to choke the attackers."

Firefighters work in a bomb-damaged street after a raid in 1941.

EMERGENCY SERVICES

A team of Civil Defence workers – firefighters, AMBULANCE crew and stretcher bearers – went to the aid of those trapped or wounded. Complete silence was needed to hear any cries for help under the rubble. Buildings could collapse at any time, and burst water, gas mains and unexploded bombs posed further risks.

Respirators were handed out during raids by civil defence workers.

> ▶ **Source: T P Peters, Reminiscences, 1945**
>
> T P Peters, an Air Raid Warden in East Grinstead, wrote about his experiences:
>
> *"Unexploded German bombs were very dangerous. The Chief Warden and I would go and inspect the holes armed with rods, to enable him to fill up the necessary forms, etc, for the Bomb Disposal Unit."*

Words to use in your project

anecdote – *a short, amusing story of history or biography*
collected – *gathered together*
gash – *a long, deep cut*
inspection – *an official examination or review*
shambles – *a place of carnage; a mess or muddle*

Glossary

ambulance – *a vehicle used for transporting sick and injured people*
apparatus – *equipment needed for a particular activity or purpose*
borough – *a term for a town, and also a district of London*
mounted – *placed on top of*
survey – *to examine carefully and thoroughly*

See also: The Raids 6–7; The Shelters 12–13; The Destruction 16–17; Work and Play 20–21

CASE STUDY

Air-raid wardens

Each London BOROUGH had teams of ARP wardens, many of who were women. Wardens worked over 72 hours a week, maintaining the blackout and checking that people had gas masks. Other duties included sounding sirens, fighting fires, giving first aid and dealing with unexploded bombs.

> ▶ **Source: T P Peters, Reminiscences, 1945**
>
> Air-raid warden T P Peters wrote:
>
> *"When the Prime Minister announced the Declaration of War … the country was well prepared with its ARP Organisation. We had received a good training from Colonel Eaton, the Chief Warden."*

A young air-raid warden in uniform.

Destruction

During the Blitz, there was huge loss of life and destruction to buildings. About two million houses were destroyed, 60,000 civilians killed and 87,000 more seriously injured.

A building wrecked after bombs rained on the capital in April, 1941.

CASUALTIES

Although the Luftwaffe targeted military and industrial sites, civilian targets were also struck to DEMORALIZE the public. Many civilians were killed when bombs hit public shelters.

Shops, businesses, schools, churches, cinemas and hospitals were destroyed. The centre of Coventry was flattened after a raid on 14 November 1940. The docks in London, Southampton, Portsmouth and Liverpool were also hit. Southampton had 2,300 bombs and 30,000 incendiary devices dropped on it, damaging and destroying 45,000 buildings.

SITE OF THE WORST CIVILIAN DISASTER OF THE SECOND WORLD WAR

IN MEMORY OF
173 MEN, WOMEN AND CHILDREN
WHO LOST THEIR LIVES ON THE
EVENING OF WEDNESDAY 3RD MARCH 1943
DESCENDING THESE STEPS TO BETHNAL GREEN
UNDERGROUND AIR RAID SHELTER

NOT FORGOTTEN

Plaque at Bethnal Green Tube Station, where 173 people lost their lives on 3 March 1943.

▶ **Sources: Manchester Guardian, 9 September 1940**

On 9 September 1940, the *Manchester Guardian* reported a bomb hitting a shelter:

"Children sleeping in PERAMBULATORS and mothers with babies in their arms were killed when a bomb exploded on a crowded shelter in an East London district during Saturday night's raids. By what is described as 'a million-to-one chance' the bomb fell directly on to a VENTILATOR shaft measuring only about three feet by one foot."

SITES AND STRUCTURES

To protect buildings, sandbags were piled outside and windows covered in tape. Camouflage was used to hide factories and churches. The final raid of the Blitz took place on London on 10 May 1941. The Houses of Parliament were hit and major railway stations damaged, as well as Westminster Abbey, St James's Palace, Lambeth Palace, the British Museum and the Central Criminal Court.

▶ **Source: Tom Hopkinson, Of This Our Time, 1982**

Tom Hopkinson wrote:

"Bombing for that year ended with the extremely heavy raid of May 10–11 in which it seemed the Germans were trying to burn down the whole of London at the same time."

Words to use in your project

alarming – *causing sudden fear or anxiety*

annihilate – *to completely destroy*

calamity – *an extreme misfortune bringing great loss and sorrow*

citizen – *a native or inhabitant of a town or city*

Glossary

demoralize – *to destroy morale*

perambulators – *baby carriages with four wheels*

spectacle – *a visually striking performance or display*

stupendous – *extremely impressive*

ventilator – *a device or appliance for airing out a room or other space*

See also: The Raids 6–7; After the Raids 14–15

CASE STUDY

London ablaze

On 29 December 1940, the Luftwaffe dropped about 100,000 incendiary bombs on central London that started 1,500 fires and killed 163 people. Firefighters used 100 million gallons of water to put out the blazes.

▶ **Source: Alan P Herbert, Memories of the Forties, 1965**

Alan P Herbert describes the scene in his book:

"The Pool, below London Bridge, was a lake of light. I saw a STUPENDOUS SPECTACLE. Half a mile or more of the Surrey shore was burning … The scene was like a lake in Hell. Burning barges were drifting everywhere … so dense was the smoke."

London burns during the Blitz.

Food and Farming

One of Germany's tactics was to cut off Britain's supplies by destroying its merchant navy, which transported goods across the Atlantic Ocean. As food imports declined, the British government ordered RATIONING and more local food to be produced.

RATIONING AND SHORTAGES

In January 1940, food rationing was introduced so that everyone received a fair share. Every family had to register with local shops to buy food. Each person's ration of sugar and bacon was only 113 grams (four ounces) of each per week. As the war went on the list of rationed foods became longer, and some foods were no longer available. People were encouraged to 'make do and mend' clothes and other items.

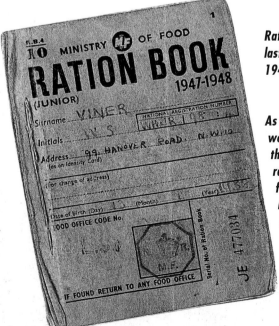

Rationing lasted from 1940–1954.

As the war went on the list of rationed foods became longer.

1940	Jan	Bacon
	Jan	Sugar
	March	Meat
	July	Tea
	July	Butter and margarine
1941	March	Jam
	May	Cheese
	June	Eggs
1942	January	Rice and dried fruits
	February	Canned tomatoes and peas
	April	Breakfast cereals and condensed milk
	July	Chocolate and sweets
	August	Biscuits
	December	Oat flakes

PRODUCING FOOD

In 1939, the 'Dig for Victory' CAMPAIGN encouraged people with gardens to produce as much food as possible. Food was grown everywhere, including ALLOTMENTS, parks, school playing fields, railway embankments, cricket pitches and even Buckingham Palace's flower beds.

> ▶ **Source: Ministry of Agriculture campaign, 1940**
>
> The 'Dig for Victory' campaign even had its own song:
>
> *'Dig! Dig! Dig! And your muscles will grow big*
> *Keep on pushing the spade*
> *Don't mind the worms*
> *Just ignore their squirms*
> *And when your back aches laugh with glee*
> *And keep on diggin'*
> *Till we give our foes a wiggin'*
> *Dig! Dig! Dig! to Victory'*

The Women's Land Army worked in the fields to help provide food.

Words to use in your project

allocate – *to distribute in shares or according to a plan*
cargo – *the load of commodities carried by a ship or aeroplane*
cultivate – *to use soil or land for growing crops*
decadent – *in a state of moral decline; self-indulgent*
emaciated – *to become abnormally lean by starvation*

Glossary

allotments – *small patches of ground used for growing food*
campaign – *a series of organized, planned actions*
coupon – *a detachable ticket, entitling the bearer to a set amount of food*
rationing – *the process of allocating a fixed amount of a material that is in short supply*

See also: Evacuation 8–9; Work and Play 20–21; Women and Children 22–23; Art 26–27

CASE STUDY

Food inspectors

During rationing people were given COUPON books to hand over when they went to buy food. Food inspectors checked that shopkeepers did not sell goods without taking the right coupons. Sometimes they worked undercover by pretending to be a customer.

> ▶ **Source: East Grinstead Observer, 16 September 1944**
>
> According to the *East Grinstead Observer*:
>
> *"Dr Frederick Ridley of Mudbrooks Farm, Forest Row, was found guilty of adding water to milk for sale. Dr Ridley was fined £15 and £3 3s costs."*

A woman uses her ration book.

Work and Play

As war was declared, the National Service Act came into force and men between 20–23 years old (18–41 after 1940), were 'called up' to join the army, navy or air force. Older or unfit men became firefighters, ARP wardens and Land Defence Volunteers (Home Guard).

THE BLITZ SPIRIT

As well as serving in the armed forces, many other important roles emerged. As men were fighting, many women took over factory work, lorry driving and farm work. Boy Scouts and Girl Guides did jobs like delivering urgent messages or making clothes. Princess Elizabeth (now Queen Elizabeth II) registered for war work three days after her 16th birthday and qualified as a driver and mechanic.

> ▶ *Source: Bishopsgate Institute committee report, October 1940*
> London's Bishopsgate Institute's librarian reported in 1940 that:
>
> *"Two members of staff – Miss Reid and Miss Daniels – have had to evacuate their homes in Stepney owing to the serious damage caused by bombs; but I am happy to state that beyond shock they are well and have loyally attended to their duties here."*

Daily life in a damaged residential neighbourhood.

PASTIMES

Despite the war, the cinema and the arts remained popular. The BBC (British Broadcasting Corporation) had stopped broadcasting television, so people read newspapers or listened to the radio for news. Cinemas also showed NEWSREELS. ENTERTAINMENT like books, dances and sports COMPETITIONS were popular, not least because they helped the community spirit. Cheap paperbacks, first introduced by Penguin Books, whiled away hours spent sheltering during air raids.

Paperback books became a popular diversion from the hardships of the war in Britain.

See also: The Blitz 4–5; Shelters 12–13; Food and Farming 18–19; Women and Children 22–23; Art 26–27

CASE STUDY

Theatre

People used the theatre as a way of forgetting their problems. The blackout meant that performances were held in the late afternoon or early evening, and rationing affected the availability of costumes and make-up. Signs were used during a performance to warn of an air raid. In London's West End, troops made up a large part of the audience, until 1941 when they were banned from taking their leave in London.

▶ **Source: Theatre World *magazine, October 1940***

Theatre World magazine wrote about these problems:

"The choice of the Londoner is now restricted to the delights of the Revudeville at the Windmill and the lunch-time ballet hour at the Arts Theatre Club, to which must be added the brave venture of Shakespeare at the Vaudeville, MATINEES only."

The Windmill was the only London theatre that remained open throughout the Blitz.

Women and Children

In 1941, women between 19 and 30 years old had to REGISTER for war work and often became drivers, mechanics or factory workers. By 1944, over 80,000 women were working on farms throughout Britain. Those in the Women's Voluntary Service (WVS) provided meals and clothing for rescue workers and those who had survived air raids.

WORKING WOMEN

By May 1943, women between the ages of 18 and 45 without children had to help with the war effort. Women drove trains, became motorcycle messengers, fought fires and worked in MUNITIONS factories. They joined the Women's Royal Naval Service (WRNS) and the Women's Royal Air Force (WRAF). They became drivers, mechanics, plane spotters and assisted on anti-aircraft guns and in operations rooms. They even became spies working behind enemy lines. The WVS operated refuge centres for people in need of help after bombing raids.

▶ **Source: Ernest Bevin's speech as reported in the Manchester Guardian, 10 March 1941**

The following is an extract from a speech by the Minister of Labour, Ernest Bevin, to persuade women to volunteer for war work:

"I have to tell the women that I cannot offer them a DELIGHTFUL life. They will have to suffer some inconveniences. But I want them to come forward in the spirit of determination to help us through."

The future Queen Elizabeth II during WWII.

CHILDREN

Many children from London were evacuated, but others who stayed witnessed the destruction of large parts of London.

Three children sit outside the wreckage of their home.

▶ **Source: Extract from an interview with Mavis Cook conducted by the Museum of London**

Mavis Cook lived in north London at the beginning of the Blitz and describes her experience:

"One evening we didn't quite make the shelter and I do recall … just just sort of lying flat because a bomb had fallen very close to the house. Everything SHUDDERED, you know, glass and everything … the whole house shook … that was the first time that I could honestly say I was very frightened …"

Words to use in your project

consequence – *a logical result*
encounter – *to meet*
occupation – *a profession*
parted – *separated*
plantation – *an estate where crops are grown*
reap – *cut or harvest grain*
restrict – *keep within certain limits*

Glossary

delightful – *charming, pleasant*
munitions – *military weapons, ammunition and stores*
register – *to enter on an official list*
shuddered – *trembled or shook*
tattie – *a name for a potato*

See also: Evacuation 8–9; Defence 10–11; Destruction 16–17; Weapons 28–29

CASE STUDY

Tattie picking

During the war, children in the country were given blue employment cards, which let them work a certain number of hours. 'Tattering' was planting potato crops in the spring. 'TATTIE picking' took place in the autumn when the harvest was ready.

▶ **Source: BBC Scotland on Film, 12 February 2003**

Margaret Strachan of Aberdeen wrote about her experiences:

"I started tattie picking for 24 shillings (£1.20) a week. The bonus was getting a free bag of the leftover tatties and carrots from the friendly farmers."

Boys of St George's Church of England School, Battersea, London, digging potatoes.

Significant People

The most SIGNIFICANT people during the war were political and military leaders, such as British Prime Minister Winston Churchill and Field Marshal Bernard Montgomery, or 'Monty'.

Sir Arthur Harris, responsible for the massive bombing campaigns in Germany.

WINSTON CHURCHILL

Winston Churchill was born on 30 November 1874. Before entering politics he worked as a war correspondent and was in the army. He was a keen amateur artist and writer who later won the Nobel Prize for Literature. He held many key government positions from 1900, before becoming prime minister on 10 May 1940 at the age of 66. Churchill had many great qualities, but he is probably best remembered for the INSPIRATIONAL speeches and public broadcasts he made to the British people.

▶ **Source: General Dwight D Eisenhower, Crusade in Europe, 1948**
American General Dwight D Eisenhower, described Winston Churchill:

"An inspirational leader, he seemed to TYPIFY Britain's courage and PERSEVERANCE in adversity and its conservatism in success. He was a man of extraordinarily strong CONVICTIONS and a master in argument and debate. Completely devoted to winning the war and discharging his responsibility …"

Winston Churchill helped to keep up morale with his famous 'V' for victory sign.

SIR ARTHUR 'BOMBER' HARRIS

Arthur Harris was born in Cheltenham on 13 April 1892. He held many positions in the RAF and was in charge of the Allied air campaign until 1945. Harris ordered 'saturation' bombing of German cities, killing over 600,000 German civilians, damaging six million homes and flattening cities.

▶ **Source: Winston Churchill, address to the House of Commons, 28 March 1945**

In 1945, Winston Churchill instructed Sir Arthur Harris to end saturation bombing. He explained:

"It seems to me that the moment has come when the question of bombing of German cities simply for the sake of increasing the terror, should be reviewed. Otherwise we shall come into control of an utterly ruined land."

CASE STUDY

'Monty'

Bernard Montgomery was born on 17 November 1887. He fought and led extensively in World War I. Following the German invasion of North Africa, Montgomery commanded the British Eighth Army in World War II. Montgomery then became Field Marshal in Europe. On 4 May 1945 he accepted the surrender of the German military.

▶ **Source: Bernard Montgomery, The Path to Leadership, 1961**

These are his own words about military leadership:

"Military command has always required technical skill and spiritual power and quality. Great commanders have had a profound knowledge of the mechanics of war and the stage-management of battle."

Field Marshal Bernard Montgomery.

Art

Many artists and photographers were paid by the Ministry of Information to record images of the war. These pictures were useful for PROPAGANDA and to bolster public morale during the war. Poets, cartoonists and authors also recorded what they saw during the war.

PAINTINGS

The War Artists' Advisory Committee was set up largely because of Kenneth Clark, who was director of the National Gallery in London. The committee employed artists to record Britain at war, and eventually took responsibility for the artistic COVERAGE of the war.

At any one time, 30 full-time artists were employed. Specific COMMISSIONS were given to another 100 artists, and the work of a further 200 artists was bought. Even more artists worked unofficially. The Committee commissioned artists including Henry Moore, Graham Sutherland and Stanley Spencer. Other artists, including the painters Anthony Gross and Edward Ardizzone, were sent to places like North Africa, Europe and the Far East, where campaigns were being fought. Exhibitions that were organized both in Britain and America aimed to raise morale and to promote Britain's image abroad.

Henry Moore made this painting during the Blitz in London, World War II.

PHOTOGRAPHY

The DEVASTATION caused by the Blitz made strong photographic images. The most famous photograph of London in the Blitz was taken from the roof of the *Daily Mail* offices in Fleet Street in December 1940, by Herbert Mason. It shows the dome of St Paul's Cathedral surrounded by fire and smoke. Despite the destruction all around, St Paul's remained intact and was a symbol of hope and determination for Londoners.

Thousands more photographs of London were taken during the war, including many NOTEWORTHY images by George Rodger, of *Life* magazine, and Bert Hardy, who worked for the popular magazine *Picture Post*.

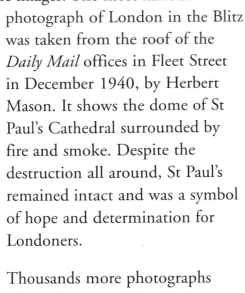

Herbert Mason's famous photo of St Paul's Cathedral during the Blitz, taken in 1940.

Words to use in your project

acclaim – *to greet with praise*
board – *a group of people who manage a business*
capacity – *the ability to contain or serve*
discover – *to find*
display – *to put something so that it can be easily seen*
historic – *relating to the past*

Glossary

commissions – *orders for something to be produced*
coverage – *the extent to which something is dealt with*
devastation – *severe shock, distress, grief or destruction*
noteworthy – *interesting, significant or unusual*
propaganda – *information usually misleading, designed to influence people's opinions*
surrealism – *an artistic movement that tried to show the workings of the inner mind*

See also: The Blitz 4–5; Work and Play 20–21; Significant People 24–25

CASE STUDY

Bill Brandt

Bill Brandt worked in Paris, France and then London, developing a style of photojournalism that captured ordinary people in their own settings. At the height of the Blitz, he took photographs of London and Londoners at different times of the day and night, and even followed crowds into the Underground to escape the bombs.

▶ **Source: Mark Haworth-Booth, 2002**

Mark Haworth-Booth, former curator of London's Victoria & Albert Museum, says:

"No other British photographer has made so many memorable photographs as Bill Brandt. He excelled in all fields – social scenes, SURREALISM, night photography, wartime documentary, landscape, portraiture and the nude."

The influential photographer Bill Brandt.

Weapons

The British and Germans used many different types of planes during the war. The RAF flew Spitfire, Defiant, Hurricane, Blenheim, Beaufighter, Lancaster and Gladiator aircraft. The Luftwaffe used Dornier, Heinkel, Messerschmitt and Junkers.

German incendiary bombs.

AIRCRAFT

The Junkers Ju 88, the Heinkel He 111 and the Dornier Do 17 were the main bombers used by the Luftwaffe during the Battle of Britain and the Blitz. However, they did not cause as much damage as the British Lancaster and the American B-17 Flying Fortress. The Junkers 88 was probably the best German PROPELLER-driven fighter.

> ▶ **Source: Sir Arthur Harris, Bomber Offensive, 1947**
> Sir Arthur Harris wrote about the Junkers 88 aircraft:
>
> *"By an almost INCREDIBLE stroke of luck the pilot of a Junkers 88 mistook England for Germany on July 13th and landed with his aircraft quite undamaged on an airfield in England. It was a Junkers 88 of the latest type and it contained two wholly new instruments for detecting aircraft in the dark."*

The Junkers Ju 88 was a four-seat bomber. It was the most versatile German warplane of the World War II era.

BOMBS

BOMBER COMMAND used three main types of bomb: target indicator, incendiary and high EXPLOSIVE. Germany used high-explosive bombs of increasing size and weight. The Luftwaffe dropped sea mines on British cities, where they became known as landmines. The Germans also introduced explosive charges with a delay of about seven minutes into some incendiary bombs.

> ▶ **Source: Extract from an interview with Joanne Shipway, conducted by the Museum of London**
> Joanne Shipway describes what it was like to live in London as a teenager during the war:
>
> *"Much of what I saw was very TRAUMATIC. German bombers not only dropped high explosive, they also dropped incendiaries so I saw horrific injuries caused by both types of bombs."*

Words to use in your project

clatter – *a rapid succession of loud noises*
harm – *to hurt or damage*
inflammable – *easily set on fire*
ordeal – *a painful experience*
ruins – *remains, wreckage*

Glossary

Bomber Command – *organization that controlled the Royal Air Force's bombers*
explosive – *likely to shatter violently*
incredible – *impossible or difficult to believe; extraordinary*
propeller – *a revolving shaft with spiral blades that makes an aircraft move*
technologically – *having to do with the application of scientific knowledge*
traumatic – *emotionally disturbing or distressing*

See also: Defence 10–11; Shelters 12–13; Women and Children 22–23

CASE STUDY

V-1/V-2

From January 1944 until 8 April, London was bombed very heavily. This time, the Germans used the V-1 bomb and the TECHNOLOGICALLY advanced V-2 rocket. The V-1 was a pilotless plane that carried a cargo of bombs to wherever it ran out of fuel. Londoners called them 'buzz bombs' or 'doodlebugs'.

> ▶ **Source: Extract from an interview with Jim Woods, conducted by the Museum of London, 1987**
> The following is an extract from an interview with Jim Wood about his experiences as a child during the war:
>
> *"The V1s were quite noisy … They sounded like a motorbike running without a silencer … and if they stopped overhead you knew they would hit close by."*

A V-1 flying bomb.

Crime

The UPHEAVAL of war created many opportunities for criminals. Looters robbed bombed-out homes and juvenile delinquents stole from people in public shelters. Rationing also led to black-market trade in restricted items like meat, alcohol and clothing.

LAW AND ORDER

The Blitz created many law and order problems. With fathers at war and mothers working, children were often not supervised and sometimes picked pockets or stole food.

With so many dying in the Blitz, even getting away with murder was possible. When the remains of a woman were found in a bombed church in 1942, the police DISCOVERED that she had been murdered. The woman's husband, Harry Dobkin, was found guilty of murder and hanged.

A 1940s policeman's lamp.

▶ **Source: Sussex and Surrey Courier, 6 January 1945**

The *Sussex and Surrey Courier* reported:

"Many cases brought before the Juvenile Courts arrive from broken homes. A lack of discipline in such homes was responsible for many of these crimes. The desire for ADVENTURE and war stories of deeds at sea, the field, and in the air, led to stealing and destructive behaviour. Gangster films and the 'tough' gangster idea also had their influence."

Hanging was the ultimate punishment for those guilty of the most serious crimes during wartime.

LOOTING AND FRAUD

Criminals made fraudulent insurance claims for bomb damage and CONCENTRATED on selling black-market goods that were difficult to obtain. Another form of crime was profiteering, in which companies made money out of supplying essential war goods. In the first week of the Blitz there were 390 cases of looting in London. Looting was punishable by death, but usually ended up in a prison sentence.

> ▶ **Source: Report by Chief Inspector Percy Datlen, Dover CID, (Criminal Investigation Department) 17 April 1942**
> Chief Inspector Percy Datlen reported what happened in Dover after one heavy raid:
>
> *"In cases where there are several houses bombed out in one street, the looters have systematically gone through the lot. Carpets have been stripped from the floors … they have even taken away heavy mangles, bedsteads and complete suites of furniture."*

Looters targeted bombed houses and businesses.

Words to use in your project

accountable – *obliged to account for one's acts*
homicide – *the killing of one human being by another*
illicit – *not allowed by law*
miscreant – *an evil person or criminal*
ransack – *to search thoroughly; plunder*

Glossary

adventure – *an unusual and exciting experience*
concentrated – *directed towards a common centre or goal*
discovered – *found out*
pickpocketing – *the act of stealing from people's pockets*
upheaval – *a major change or disruption*

See also: The Blitz 4–5; After the Raids 14–15; Destruction 16–17; Work and Play 20–21; Women and Children 22–23

CASE STUDY

Blackout gangs

Gangs of teenagers were often blamed for PICKPOCKETING and stealing people's belongings in crowded air-raid shelters. Some also stole from gardens, while others burgled houses.

> ▶ **Source: Colonel Henriques, Clerkenwell Magistrates Court, 24 October 1940**
> While sentencing a 15-year-old boy for burgling a house, magistrate Colonel Henriques said:
>
> *"It is becoming more and more common. It is just playing dirty in wartime."*

Teenage gangs would steal the bags of people sleeping in shelters like this one.

Index

World War II & The Blitz Timeline

September 1939
Britain declares war on Germany after its invasion of Poland. The first wave of children are evacuated from the cities to the countryside.

January 1940
Rationing introduced into Britain. It lasts for nearly 14 years.

May 1940
Winston Churchill becomes prime minister of Britain.

September 1940
The Blitz begins 7 September and continues on until 1942, with German air attacks on London, Coventry and other cities.

December 1940
German bombing campaign known as the 'Christmas Raids' leads to another wave of evacation of children.

December 1941
National Service is enacted. WVS and many other organizations are created.

June 1943
Allies begin round-the-clock bombing raids over Germany.

January 1944
More air attacks by Germany are followed by V-1 or pilotless flying bombs.

June 1944
The D-Day invasion of Europe begins on the beaches of Normandy, northern France.

May 1945
Germany surrenders unconditionally to the Allies. Adolf Hitler has already commited suicide.

August 1945
The Americans drop atom bombs on the cities of Hiroshima and Nagaski in Japan to end WWII.